A souvenir guide

Montacute House
Somerset

Nicholas Cooper and Jo Moore

National Trust

National Portrait Gallery

Glittering Glass and Golden Stone

Montacute is one of the loveliest of English houses.

The honey-coloured, Ham Hill stone of its two faultless façades glows in the morning and afternoon sun. It is satisfyingly large but not overwhelmingly grand; its rooms seem dignified but comfortable at the same time. Like every old house Montacute has been altered over the years, but these changes seem only to make it more human. It is many people's favourite.

'By far the most beautiful house of middle size in England.'

Lord Curzon on Montacute

New money and new men

Montacute was probably begun around 1595 and finished by 1601, at the very end of the reign of Queen Elizabeth and at the height of an extraordinary period of country-house building.

There were already several other impressive houses within fifteen miles – Barrington, Brympton, Clifton Maybank, Hinton St George and Sherborne New Castle, and many others like Lytes Cary and Sandford Orcas that approach these in size and status. Under the Tudor monarchs there were many new fortunes to be made – from the estates which had formerly belonged to the monasteries dissolved by Henry VIII, from burgeoning trade and commerce, from service to the State, and – partly through the business arising out of all of these – from the law. When the only reliable investment was in land, and when landowning brought prestige, authority and solid wealth to hand down to one's heirs, it was natural, indeed expected, that those who had made fortunes should seek the status proclaimed by a fine new house.

Offered 'for scrap' in 1931, Montacute was rescued for the National Trust as one of its first great houses, and is now filled with furniture, fine tapestries, and Tudor and Jacobean portraits on loan from the National Portrait Gallery.

Left The east front

Above Nearby Barrington Court (also in the care of the National Trust) has many similarities to Montacute

The Phelipses: The rise and fall of a county family

The first Edward Phelips (1560?–1614), for whom Montacute was built, was a typical man of his age. His father, grandfather and great-grandfather had been gradually building up their wealth since the late 15th century, acquiring profitable jobs in the service of greater men, in local administration and as collectors of customs and taxes, and prudently buying property with the gains they made.

A century later, the Phelipses were well established among the gentry of Somerset and Dorset. When Edward's father, Thomas, died in 1588, it was at Montacute that Edward Phelips decided to settle.

By then he was already advancing his own fortunes. Trained as a lawyer and entering Parliament in 1584, by 1604 he was Speaker of the House of Commons. Legal appointments in royal service (which included prosecuting the Gunpowder Plotters) culminated in his becoming Master of the Rolls – the second most senior judge in England – in 1608. He had been knighted by James I in 1603, and in building his new house he had been doing what was expected of a man in his position.

Left Sir Edward Phelips I, the builder of Montacute

However, in a highly competitive age, living up to one's rank cost money. Edward Phelips died relatively young and £12,000 in debt. His son Robert also entered Parliament, where he was extremely active in opposing King James and, later, Charles I. Such opposition may have been principled, but not wise; it earned him no well-paid appointments, made him enemies locally as well as nationally, and in his keen politicking he seems to have neglected his own affairs and his family obligations. When Robert Phelips died in 1638, Montacute was grandly – perhaps luxuriously – furnished, but over the next twenty years his son Edward II seems to have sold much of the house's contents. Not only were there family obligations of £1200 to pay, but also his own fine of £1300 for fighting on the Royalist side in the Civil War.

Left Sir Robert Phelips MP, who was active against the King in Parliament (National Portrait Gallery)

Above Col. Edward Phelips II, who was a Royalist officer in the Civil War

Undistinguished and in debt

None of the later Phelipses achieved the distinction of the first Edward, or even of his son.

The third Edward Phelips (1638–99) was undistinguished as MP for Somerset, and as a county magistrate was chiefly known for his zealous prosecution of religious nonconformists. Leaving three daughters and a house whose grandest room was apparently bare of furnishings, Edward Phelips III might have lost the family estates then, had not two daughters in succession – Ann and Elizabeth – married their cousin, Edward Phelips IV (1678–1734), reuniting separated sections of family property.

Despite the wealth that these two women brought to the estate, the fifth Edward Phelips (1725–97) inherited debts of £22,000, and Montacute was only saved by his widowed mother Elizabeth's wise estate management during his minority and in due course by fortunate inheritances from relatives. Such an improved financial situation saved the family, and also allowed them to alter the Elizabethan house.

The work of Edward Phelips V (1725–97) in the 1780s is described on p.15. Further restorations and sales of contents over the next 70 years reflected periodic changes in taste and fluctuating family circumstances. Of much of this work, little is recorded; some has been swept away, and some may still be unrecognised.

Above left to right
Sir Edward Phelips III, who was MP for Somerset;

Edward Phelips IV;

Elizabeth Phelips was the daughter of Edward Phelips III. She married her cousin Edward Phelips IV and by her careful management of the estate saved Montacute for her son, Edward Phelips V (the boy standing on the left)

William Phelips (1823–89), who inherited in 1834, came of age in 1844. He married a rich woman, Ellen Helyar, in the following year. He also commissioned an ambitious architectural scheme which would have made Montacute into a wild Victorian parody of an Elizabethan house. Although, fortunately, little of this was carried out, much redecoration was done. However, his extravagance and his gambling once more depleted the family wealth, and from around 1860 his mental instability was such that the estates had to be managed by his brother.

Challenging times

In 1875 the management of the family's estates was assumed by William Phelips's son, William Robert Phelips. Financially, this was a challenging time for him to take it on. Like many other landowners, the Phelipses were almost certainly hit hard by the depression that struck English agriculture from the late 1870s and continued with only a short break until 1940. The income that had supported the household in the prosperous heyday of 19th-century farming, and that had probably allowed William Phelips to borrow money against the value of his estates, would have fallen considerably by the end of the century, along with the price of land itself. It would soon be clear that the cost of maintaining the house and the establishment of servants that it demanded was beyond the family's means. In 1913 – ironically, on the eve of a temporary boom in land values with the First World War – William Robert decided that he could not go on. Over the next few years estate farms were gradually sold, while the house itself was leased out.

Above left to right
Edward Phelips V, who rebuilt the west front;

William Phelips with Montacute in the background;

William Robert Phelips

1913–25.
The leaseholders

Robert Davidson

Robert Davidson's career had been in the east, and his interest in Montacute was mainly for the shooting. Unsurprisingly, he complained loudly about the state of the cooking and heating apparatus and the defective drains and plumbing – all inadequate but all essential for the entertainment of shooting parties. In any event, his tenancy did not last long, and in 1915 the house was leased to George Nathaniel Curzon, Lord Curzon of Kedleston.

Lord Curzon

Curzon was highly cultivated, extremely rich, and had already had a formidable career in politics and as Viceroy of India from 1899 to 1905. He was scathing about the state of Montacute when he took the house and refused to accept any of the Phelipses' furnishings. Later he wrote that it had been 'converted by me into a stately Jacobean mansion instead of a bad mid-Victorian villa,' but that he had 'no aspiration to fill the place with costly things, imported or fabricated or reproduced, as I have seen too frequently done elsewhere … The bulk of the Elizabethan furniture which I placed in the interior I collected from old towns and villages in the neighbourhood.' Nonetheless, he altered rooms, restored woodwork, referred to 'my irremovable wallpapers and silks', and reckoned that he had spent at least £25,000 (well over a million pounds in current values) on suitable furniture and redecoration. To judge from the auction details when some of his furnishings were dispersed in two two-day sales in 1929, they were a great deal grander than Curzon had described them.

Above Lord Curzon, who rented Montacute from 1915; after John Singer Sargent, 1914 (National Portrait Gallery)

Left Lord Curzon's Bedroom. Curzon installed the bath

More work of art than home

Curzon's motives in leasing Montacute when he already had houses of his own, were probably in part the opportunity to perfect a house from a period he admired, partly a relaxing occupation for his extremely active mind, and partly to acquire a house where he could visit his mistress, the romantic novelist Elinor Glyn (who may initially have had a hand in the decoration herself). How much of his time Curzon actually spent there is uncertain; deeply involved in government during the war and in the post-war settlement, he may have seen his work at Montacute more as the creation of a work of art than of a home. In any case, he was not there in 1916, when Elinor Glyn famously learned about his engagement to his second wife by reading about it in *The Times,* burnt 500 of his letters and walked out.

No buyer

Curzon died in 1925. Edward Phelips, who had inherited in 1918 and realised he would never live at Montacute himself, would have put it on the market at once had not Curzon's widow still had six years to run of her husband's lease. Edward Phelips died in 1928, and his brother Gerard, a bachelor who lived in Canada, immediately began negotiations to buy out Lady Curzon's interest and to sell the house. Yet again the timing was unfortunate. Stripped of the Curzon furniture and the Phelipses' own possessions (including very many of the family portraits) and placed on the market on the eve of the great depression, Montacute found no buyer. It would be three more years before the house was finally sold, together with what remained of its estate.

Above The parrot wallpaper was put up by Lord Curzon

Right The romantic novelist Elinor Glyn

ERNEST E. COOK
Montacute House 1931
Bath Assembly Rooms 1931
Buscot Park 1949
Coleshill 1956

1931. Salvation: Ernest Cook and the National Trust

In 1931 Montacute and the remainder of the Phelips property were bought for the National Trust by Ernest Cook of Thomas Cook travel agents.

Montacute was only the second country house acquired by the Trust. (By coincidence, Barrington Court, nearby and almost a prototype of Montacute, had been the first.) The price paid was £29,000, but this included the remaining land and many of the cottages in the village. These had been seriously neglected, and over the next seven years they and the house itself were slowly put back in order for the Trust by the Society for the Protection of Ancient Buildings. But money remained short, the SPAB had to lend the Trust the cost of repairs, and the house remained empty. In the first year in the National Trust's ownership, Montacute was visited by just 1822 people. In 1934 would-be visitors were told that the house would be open 'on application, at all reasonable hours', but only until a tenant had been found. It was still hoped that

somebody could be persuaded to live in the house and maintain it. The Trust seems only slowly to have realised that they were unlikely to find a tenant and that it would have to make something of Montacute itself. Management of the house was assumed by the Trust from the SPAB in 1938, on the eve of the Second World War: not the best time to plan its long-term future.

Above The plasterwork overmantel in the Library

Opposite Ernest Cook, who helped to rescue Montacute

The Form of the House

Montacute is typical of its age in combining the up-to-date with the traditional.

1601. Edward Phelips I's house

The east front – originally the entrance front, which visitors would have seen first – followed the latest fashions: completely symmetrical, with a decorative roof line of chimneys and shaped gables, and three storeys of great windows.

The novelty of symmetry

When it was built, the idea that a large house should have a symmetrical front was still quite new – such symmetry was scarcely known before around 1580, although houses had been evolving towards such symmetry for some time. Barrington, built around 1555 a few miles away, is very like Montacute in its layout and can be seen as a forerunner in that its façade is almost symmetrical, but not quite. The regular lines of windows at Montacute are not just an essential part of the design but also advertise Edward Phelips's wealth. Light and heat cost money – heat because of the cold from great windows, light because of the cost of glass.

The east front

The east front of Montacute is symmetrical, but it is very far from dull and the more one examines it, the more satisfying and sophisticated a composition it seems to be. There is a subtle rhythm of large and still larger windows, and projections that enliven the façade without breaking it up. The top floor is punctuated by a regular line of niches with figures, which vary the ornament while maintaining the scale. Between the central porch and the north and south wings, the central elevation is formed of two matching sections, each symmetrical in itself about a projecting bay.

The Nine Worthies

External decoration is very restrained, comprising little more than the roof line and the figures in the niches. These represent the Nine Worthies, long established folk heroes, three from the Bible, three from the ancient world and three from the Middle Ages. They are depicted in Roman dress simply because their sculptor would not have known how else to indicate their antiquity.

A traditional plan

Montacute's plan is conservative, and goes back to the Middle Ages. For centuries houses were effectively in two parts – the 'high' end, with the best rooms, and the 'low' end containing the kitchens and other service rooms. At the centre of the house lay the hall. Montacute preserves this traditional layout, even though it was increasingly unsuited to the practical needs of the Elizabethan household. Once, a hall had been the common room for the entire household and a place for occasional gatherings of everyone in the community. By 1600 it survived chiefly as a symbol of the owner's status, used solely as the entrance to the house and as the dining room for servants, except on occasions such as Christmas dinner or harvest suppers, when the whole household and perhaps tenants might still celebrate together. Nor was this long, narrow plan, with the centre of the house a single room deep, particularly convenient. In a large house it meant that service rooms were a long way from family rooms, and that without separate internal corridors, one had to pass through intermediate rooms to get from one end of the house to the other.

Above Montacute adopted a traditional plan with the hall at the centre of the house

Opposite The east front

William Arnold

Montacute was almost certainly designed and built by the master mason, William Arnold.

In 1600 the profession of architect had not yet emerged; buildings were designed by the man who undertook the building, drawing on his own practical experience and knowledge and on the wishes of the owner. If the owner moved in the upper levels of society or was highly educated, he might well have seen more great houses than the master mason himself. If he was interested in such things, he might also have seen architectural books from abroad.

There is no direct confirmation that William Arnold was the designer and builder of Montacute, but it is highly likely. Arnold may have learnt his craft at Longleat in the 1570s, at the time the most architecturally advanced house in England. When Dorothy Wadham was preparing for the building of Wadham College in Oxford in 1610 in fulfilment of her dead husband's will, Edward Phelips had recommended 'one Arnold... an honest man, a perfectt workman', who was given the contract. Montacute incorporates certain highly distinctive decorative details, which appear also at Cranborne Manor in Dorset. Cranborne belonged to Robert Cecil, the Lord Treasurer, who in the same year had been consulting Arnold over new work, 'every day a whole houre in private.'

Cecil's interest in architecture is well documented; his employment of Arnold is the highest commendation. The most notable of the details that the two houses share are shell-headed niches with the whorl of the shell at the top rather than – as usual – at the base, and richly decorated overmantels ornamented with a half frame of strapwork rather than – again, as was more usual – a complete frame. Arnold's home was at Charlton Musgrove, a little north-east of Wincanton, and he may also have had a professional involvement with the Ham Hill quarries. It is reasonable to think that these idiosyncratic details, which occur nowhere else save in some other houses in the region, are either his own or those of craftsmen working very closely with him.

Above The shell-headed niches are a decorative feature shared with Cranborne Manor, which was designed by William Arnold, who probably also built Montacute

Later alterations

It is easy to believe, from its very perfection, that Montacute is unaltered. In fact this is far from the case, and there have been significant changes both outside and inside.

The east front – the original entrance front – does indeed remain as it was designed and built, apart from the loss of the gatehouse and outer courtyard, and the simplification of the remaining inner front courtyard.

A new west front

The west side, however, was transformed in 1786, when Edward Phelips V changed the main entrance from east to west. He created a long drive centred on the new entrance, and gave the house itself a new west front by removing and rebuilding here the original façade of Clifton Maybank, a neighbouring house built around 1555. Over the porch Edward Phelips retained the diamond-shaped frame, within which the arms of Sir John Horsey combined Gothic and very early Renaissance motifs. There are similar coats of arms on some other local houses, and they must all be the work of the same mason – perhaps an immigrant bringing the latest style from France.

Why was the west front altered?

The purpose of this new addition was threefold. One was to dignify the new approach to what, until then, had probably been a relatively plain front overlooking a service area. The second was to allow a long corridor to be formed in the space between the original west front of the house and the new façade, so as to make it easier to go from one end of the house to the other.

The third was to achieve all this without building something that would look discordantly modern. By transplanting the front of another ancient house – in fact, one that was even older – Montacute's character could be preserved and enhanced. To add an addition in a similar or sympathetic style to an ancient house was at the time highly unusual, although it would become normal practice a generation later. It is a pity that we do not know who Edward Phelips V's architect might have been, and that he left nothing to indicate his own thoughts on the matter.

The corridor that ran the length of the new façade made it possible to re-plan the interior. Over the years, more internal alterations followed, mainly decorative but in some cases involving the further moving of partitions and re-organisation of interior spaces. Some of these involved significant losses or changes to original plasterwork and panelling. Others were done so skilfully as to make it uncertain, two centuries on, exactly what work was undertaken, and there may still be discoveries to make. Certainly, for a very long time people have believed that what they were seeing was an unaltered Elizabethan house, when in fact Montacute, like almost every other old house, has changed with the needs and tastes of its occupants.

Above **The Clifton Maybank Corridor runs the entire length of the house, allowing easier circulation**

Below left In 1786 Edward Phelips V remodelled the west front to incorporate 16th-stonework from nearby Clifton Maybank

The Rooms of the House
The ground floor

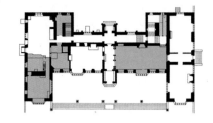

The Great Hall

Visitors entered the house, as they still do, at the 'low' end of the hall, into an open passage divided from the body of the room by a screen, which by its decoration gave visitors an immediate impression of Edward Phelips's wealth. Originally, the room would have been quite plainly furnished; in everyday use, it was the entry and the room where the servants took their daily meals.

The most notable features in the room are the screen, and the plasterwork frieze at the far ('high') end. The screen, almost certainly designed by William Arnold, is of two contrasting stones (it had been painted all over brown when Curzon arrived; he made William Robert Phelips strip it). The rams' heads on the capitals are derived from a pattern-book by the Netherlands engraver Vredeman de Vries – a source of ornamental detail widely used in late Elizabethan and Jacobean decoration.

A humiliated husband

At the far end is a plaster frieze depicting a 'skimmington' – a traditional, public humiliation for a henpecked husband who, in allowing his wife to get the better of him (for instance, by making him look after the baby), disturbed what was felt to be the proper, patriarchal ordering of society. There are other contemporary houses where the hall carries lessons for the servants, but few where they are as graphic as they are at Montacute.

Alterations

There have been significant alterations. Originally, there would have been a dais – a raised platform – at the 'high' end. In the Middle Ages, this would have been where the lord took his meals, raised a little above the level of the servants in the body of the room, and a dais survived in Elizabethan houses simply as a symbol of his authority. This was probably removed in the late 18th century, when a blue lias and ham stone floor was laid down, which survives beneath the present floor boards. Probably at the same time, the stone doorways were formed at either end. Although these look convincingly Tudor, they must actually be of *c.*1786, when the Clifton Maybank west front was added. (The fact that they are aligned on the axis of the room is characteristic of Georgian planning, but completely at variance with Elizabethan practice. Nor would the Elizabethans have made a passage that led from the centre of the dais directly to the garden.) The panelling on the west (fireplace) wall has been altered where, before the addition of the Clifton Maybank Corridor, there had been windows.

At the west end of the screens passage there are two porches, inner and outer. The outer porch is part of the Clifton Maybank work; the inner porch is probably of 1600. High up towards its ceiling are some very attractive heraldic beasts that must have formed part of the original ornament either of Clifton Maybank or of Montacute itself.

Above **The Great Hall**

Opposite **The ram heads on the Great Hall screen are copied from a Netherlandish pattern-book**

The ground floor

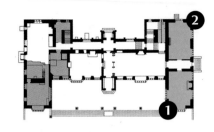

1. The Parlour

When the house was built, the Parlour was the family's principal living and dining room, and where, save on special occasions, they would have entertained their close friends. The Ham stone chimneypiece is original to the room, as are the panelling and the plaster frieze with its charming figures of animals alternating with heraldry. The ceiling, in a Jacobean style, is 19th-century.

Alterations

The main alterations to the Parlour have been to the entrance, which probably originally opened off the Great Hall dais into the south-west corner, and on the south side. Here the Victorians filled in a window bay to make a sideboard recess. The hound chasing a hare and a fox in the section of frieze that was inserted here may reflect William Phelips's love of hunting.

Above The Parlour

Below The original plaster frieze in the Parlour alternates heraldry with animals

2. The Drawing Room

The Drawing Room may have been intended as a ground-floor bedroom when first built, but it has been enlarged – probably by taking in another room to its east – and preserves nothing of its original decoration. In the course of its history, the room seems to have had no fewer than five different chimneypieces. The existing chimneypiece is of c.1655, salvaged from Coleshill, tragically burnt down in 1952; it carries the monogram of the Earl of Radnor who had lived there. Installed by the National Trust, this replaces one introduced by Curzon, which itself replaced a highly ornamented Victorian one inserted by William Robert Phelips. That probably replaced a Georgian one, which in turn replaced the original of 1600.

The wallpaper was put up by the National Trust, on the recommendation of John Fowler, the interior decorator who did much work for the Trust in the 1950s and '60s.

Below The Drawing Room

The ground floor

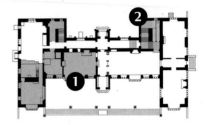

1. The Dining Room

As it appears now, the Dining Room is the work of Edward Phelips V in 1786 and Lord Curzon after 1915.

Before the addition of the new corridor behind the Clifton Maybank façade, the southern part of the central range followed a very traditional plan. Immediately south of the hall and opening off it was the Buttery, where bread and beer were kept for the servants and for casual visitors. This was probably undecorated and unheated, and would have contained a stair down to a beer cellar beneath. Beyond this lay two or three other secondary rooms, perhaps a pantry and a bedchamber for a butler. Linking the hall to the south wing, down the west side of the central range, was a service passage, providing access to these rooms that it passed and ending at the kitchens.

Alterations

The first major alteration was when the Clifton Maybank Corridor made it possible to do away with the old service passage and throw the space into the rooms it passed. This also enabled chimneys to be built to heat these ground-floor rooms on their west side. Accordingly, Edward Phelips V made the old Buttery into a family dining room. This has a fireplace with the Phelips arms dated 1599, which he probably moved from elsewhere in the house, and panelling which he may have brought down here from an upstairs chamber. At the same time he removed the original cellar stair.

The second major change was when Lord Curzon doubled the size of the room – too small for the parties he wanted to entertain – by removing the partition between it and the room beyond and extending the panelling round the walls. Much of this added panelling was probably brought in by him, but it blends well with what was installed in the 1780s. The small fireplace that formerly heated the further room, probably put in by the Victorians, remained in place so that the Dining Room now has two.

The south wing

The south wing contains the kitchen, bakehouse and other service rooms, perhaps originally including what would have been called a Low Parlour (from its being at the 'low' end of the house) or a Winter Parlour (from its being near the kitchens for warmth and so that food did not have far to travel). This would have been a small, informal, family room for daily meals. Such a room was a normal feature in any substantial house, and Montacute almost certainly had one. It may have been the southernmost room of the central range; alternatively, it was the eastern room of the south wing, which was otherwise probably a lodging chamber for guests (not open to visitors).

2. The Stairs

Montacute has two grand, formal flights of stone stairs almost equal in size, one adjacent to each wing. The arrangement closely follows the plan of Wimbledon House, built in Surrey in the 1580s, which Edward Phelips I probably knew from his close links with government and from the time he will have spent in London. The reason for there being two is that since the central range was long and narrow, with no original passages on the first floor, the upper floors of each end of the house had to be separately accessible. It was not until the building of the Clifton Maybank Corridor that this inconvenience was overcome.

Opposite **The Dining Room**

Right **The Stairs**

The first floor

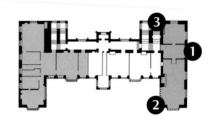

1. The Lobby

This provides access from the stair landing to the rooms either side. The doorways, now central to these rooms, were probably repositioned here in the 18th century. In the 19th century the space was known as the Armoury, from the display of weapons and armour hung on the walls.

2. The Library (Great Chamber)

The main reception rooms at Montacute were the same as those in any grand house of the time: a Great Chamber, primarily for dining and formal parties; a Withdrawing Chamber beyond it, where those who had been entertained in the Great Chamber could relax, talk, play games or carry on drinking after dinner; and a best bedroom for distinguished guests.

What is now the Library was Edward Phelips I's Great Chamber. In 1699 the room had apparently been empty; in 1728 it was a lumber room. At some time before the existing panelling was inserted, the room had been hung with a red flock paper.

The room has its original chimneypiece, similar in its details to other work by William Arnold, and there were formerly naked figures of nymphs or goddesses standing in the niches. William Phelips's wife thought they were indecent, and had them taken out to the garden where they were destroyed by frost.

The panelling was copied from that in the Parlour and was probably installed in the early 19th century. The bookcases were put in a little later.

Left The Library

The plaster frieze all round the room, with deep, square, decorative panels, is repeated in the Withdrawing Room and in the bedchamber beyond. There are a number of irregularities in these friezes, the result of repairs at various dates and the need to remodel them when partitions were moved or inserted and windows blocked, but the intention may always have been to give these state rooms a unified scheme of decoration.

3. Lord Curzon's Bedroom

The walls may have originally been hung with gilt leather, but Curzon added further panelling to what he probably found there already. He also installed a bath, enclosed with old wainscot that had previously formed a cupboard in the kitchen. Over the fireplace is a simple plaster figure of the Old Testament King of Israel, David, with his harp.

Above **Lord Curzon's Bedroom**

Right **Heraldic stained glass decorates the windows of the Library**

A grand draught excluder

The splendid wind porch in the Library – an internal panelled porch to help keep out the draughts – may originally have been in the corner of the Parlour downstairs. It had been removed from there in the 19th century, and Lord Curzon found it in pieces round the house and had it restored and moved here. The full significance of the Latin inscription *'Hoc Age'* – 'Do This' – is a puzzle, but the Elizabethans liked moral lessons and injunctions of every kind, and it may simply be urging the reader to get on with things rather than sitting around: a sound maxim for a successful man like the first Edward Phelips.

The first floor

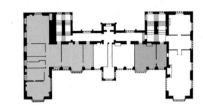

The Crimson Dressing Room and Bedroom

These rooms were originally a single space – the Withdrawing Room to the Great Chamber of Edward Phelips I. They were probably a bedroom from the 18th century.

Like the Library, it seems for some time before the 18th century to have been unused. These rooms are now entered from the Clifton Maybank Corridor, but were originally reached directly from the Great Chamber – now the Library – by a doorway which Curzon rediscovered and then covered up again.

Decoration

The rooms still retain a good deal of their original decoration. The plaster frieze resembles that in the Great Chamber; the panelling on the walls is largely original. But more panelling had to be found or made up for the new partition when the room was divided; some of this looks old and re-used, while some is very plain to save the expense of elaborate carving in what was only a dressing room. Similarly, the plaster frieze had to be reproduced when the new partition was made to divide the rooms.

Fireplace and frieze

Otherwise, the chief alteration was to the fireplace, which has been altered more than once. This must have originally been central to the Withdrawing Room's west wall, and when the new dressing room was made it was necessary to move it so that it would not be right in the corner of the new bedroom. However, it could not be moved to the centre of the new room because of the need to use the existing chimney flue. Above it in the frieze, but not directly above, is a plaster panel depicting the Judgement of Paris (whose choice between three Greek goddesses precipitates the Trojan wars). This was probably moved there in the course of an earlier scheme of redecoration, before the room was divided into two. The existing fireplace surround looks Tudor, but was almost certainly inserted by Curzon. An old photograph shows a simple, early Victorian surround here.

Right The Crimson Bedroom

Left The plaster frieze in the Crimson Bedroom depicts the Judgement of Paris

The first floor

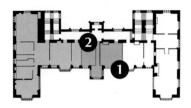

1. The Hall Chamber

The Hall Chamber was originally the best bedchamber, leading off the Withdrawing Room before the Clifton Maybank Corridor was added.

In 1638 the walls were hung with tapestry, possibly above panelling. If so, the panelling that Edward Phelips V put up in the Dining Room in 1786 may have come from here. The fireplace is original, but the reason why it is not in the centre is that the room formerly extended further to the south, with closets above the east and west porches.

The present south wall was inserted by Curzon, to allow the users of other bedrooms to reach the bathroom that he installed above the east porch. Curzon inserted the door surround leading through this wall and also added a surround to the door in the west wall, in both cases mixing new wood carving with fragments of old.

At some unknown date the room was further subdivided. Scars in the cornice on each side of the room, on the ceiling and a break in the floorboards show where a partition has been removed.

Left **The Hall Chamber**

Right **The plasterwork overmantel in the Hall Chamber**

2. The Brown Room

Another much-altered room, formed out of part of the original Hall Chamber and part of the former room beyond it. The enlargement shows most clearly in the frieze on the east wall, where there is a clear break between the northern and southern parts. The present fireplace was inserted by Curzon, with a patent grate; the carefully written instructions inside a cupboard door to the right explaining how to use it are typical of his minute attention to detail.

The further rooms

Beyond the Brown Room lay further chambers, many of which have been altered at various times. It is likely that Edward Phelips I's own bedchamber was above the kitchen at the western end of the south wing, a normal location whereby the house's owner could benefit from the warmth below. The chamber at the eastern end of the south wing is said to have been fitted up for Lady Curzon, perhaps after her husband's death in 1925 and before she surrendered her lease three years later: it has a spectacular plaster ceiling, copied from one in the Reindeer Inn at Banbury in Oxfordshire, and blank panels over the fireplace perhaps for coats of arms that were never installed. Lord Curzon decorated the smaller bedrooms in the south wing for his three daughters, Irene, Alexandra and Cimmie, and installed a bathroom for their use. These are now used as offices by the National Trust.

The second floor

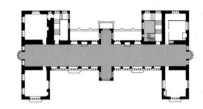

The Gallery

A gallery was an essential component in any upper-class Elizabethan house. It was a space for exercise and entertainment, where family members and guests could walk the length of the house, enjoying the views from the windows as well as the portraits that demonstrated the family's connections and loyalties.

The Montacute Gallery runs from north to south and was originally panelled. Its great length

called for two fireplaces to heat the space, though the existing fireplaces and the flanking panelling are 20th-century replacements. The original form of the ceiling is not known, though John Phelips in the early 19th century sought to improve its appearance by removing the tie beams of the roof; as a result, the walls of the house began to be pushed outwards and had to be restrained by the iron ties which bind the roof now. There are bedchambers off each end of the Gallery, intended for visitors or for members of the family. Later these probably became servants' rooms; and later still, Curzon had them fitted up for visitors, with narrow bathrooms between these bedrooms and the Gallery.

The importance of the Montacute Gallery led to the creation of a partnership between the National Trust and the National Portrait Gallery that allows for the display of Tudor and Jacobean portraits in an appropriate architectural context. The Gallery was first opened to the public in 1975 after a two-year project of renovation under the guidance of John Fowler. A subsequent redecoration in 1999 and re-display of the portraits further strengthened the partnership, and the changing displays in the rooms off the Gallery continue to be hugely popular.

Left The bay windows at the ends of the Gallery offer spectacular views over the garden

Right The Gallery

The Collection

The story of the acquisition of the objects at Montacute, from its opening to the public in 1931, when it was virtually empty of contents, to its current internationally significant collection, is a unique and extraordinary one.

James Lees-Milne, the Historic Buildings Secretary for the National Trust at the time, understood the challenges which had been taken on with the acquisition of this building and called it an 'empty and rather embarrassing white elephant'. During the Second World War the house was requisitioned and used as safe storage for the collections of the Victoria & Albert Museum, deemed too at risk to remain in London. At the end of the war, when Montacute re-opened to the public, it was clear that something needed to be done to increase visitor numbers and revive both house and garden. Planning for this major undertaking was done by Lees-Milne and Eardley Knollys, the Trust's District Agent. Interiors were redecorated and planting was completed in the garden.

The birth of the collection

When Montacute was handed over to the National Trust at a formal ceremony on 11 June 1931, it was virtually empty of contents – the result of several major sales over the years.

The ceremony in the garden was followed by a tour of the house, in which 'hardly a stick of furniture was anywhere to be seen'. Unfurnished, except for some Phelips family portraits, the house was opened to the public in 1932. Few people visited the house in the following years. After the Second World War, in 1945, the Victoria & Albert Museum transported its stored items back to London and the house was returned by the Ministry of Works to the National Trust.

The idea to make Montacute a furnished house, as opposed to a museum, marked a brave new step for the Trust. Under the name 'Silk Purses Ltd', a distinguished committee was set up, with the initial aim of furnishing seven rooms at Montacute, with the Long Gallery only being opened on request. Two people were the driving force behind this ambitious project – James Lees-Milne and Eardley Knollys. Together, with ingenuity, courage and huge energy, they set about the task.

Beginning with the letter in *The Times,* the response was good. The first offer was made on 12 April, the day after the article was published, and a further 30 followed in the next eight months. Despite some notable exceptions, however, the committee felt disappointed by the quality of many of the other pieces.

MONTACUTE HOUSE

TO THE EDITOR OF THE TIMES

Sir,—May I, as chairman of the National Trust, crave the hospitality of your columns to put before your readers an aspect of our work to which we attach increasing importance? It may be illustrated by the case of Montacute House, Somerset, where we desire to add to the interest and attraction of the building by furnishing some of the rooms. Later, if the offer of suitable furnishings is forthcoming, and the number of visitors encouraging, we propose to establish there a country museum, somewhat on the lines of Temple Newsam.

Our first step will be to furnish five or six of the principal apartments. We need for a start a few pieces of first-class quality in order to give the rooms something of the character they had during the first century after the house was built, and this letter is an invitation to members of the public to offer us as gifts, or on loan, suitable furniture, carpets, and other *objets d'art* for this purpose. At present we confine our invitation to pieces made before the year 1700, but we make no restriction on their origin, though pieces derived from the West Country would be of special interest. We feel that many people who are moving into smaller houses may like to know that some fine piece, for which they no longer have space, will in this way be cared for in perpetuity by the National Trust, and be well displayed for the enjoyment of visitors to this historic house, regarded by the late Lord Curzon as being by far the most beautiful house of middle size in England.

It may be possible, at a later date, to extend the scheme to other houses belonging to the Trust. In that case gifts would be regarded as being interchangeable as between the houses, so as to secure the best possible setting and variety of interest for visitors.

Offers should be made by letter addressed: The Secretary, Montacute Committee, National Trust, 7, Buckingham Palace Gardens, London, S.W.1.

Yours faithfully,

ZETLAND.

'Letter to the editor'
A letter to the editor of *The Times,* published on 11 April 1945, from Lord Zetland, Chairman of the National Trust, appealed for help with furnishing Montacute with pieces dated before 1700.

Opposite far left James Lees-Milne

Opposite left Eardley Knollys; photographed in 1924 by Lady Ottoline Morrell (National Portrait Gallery)

Left In the early National Trust years, the whole house was as barely furnished as the Stairs

The development of the collection

A second appeal in February 1946, this time in the form of a letter to about 50 surrounding country house owners and extending the date of desired pieces to 1760, again had a good response in terms of numbers (over 40 offers were made during that year), but again many were deemed unsuitable.

The initial aims for the standard of items accepted were never compromised, despite the unpromising background of post-war austerity of the time, when money was tight, and the challenges of fuel shortages made even the inspection of potential acquisitions and their subsequent delivery to the house very difficult. Montacute reopened to visitors in July 1946, after being closed for seven years, with the entrance fee set at one shilling per person. 8,759 people visited the house over the next four months: a great success. Today the annual number of visitors is over 120,000.

Despite such a successful start, it was recognised that many years would be needed to furnish the house to a suitable standard, and the committee continued to meet every few months. In March 1946 James Lees-Milne recorded that he spent the day 'arranging the few inadequate pieces of furniture so far collected. Did not make much of a show...'. However, new pieces continued to arrive and, a few months later, he felt that 'daylight is beginning to appear on the dusky horizon'.

In addition to items offered by individual people, others were acquired in different ways.

Suitable contents from Brockhampton House, added to the Trust's holdings in 1946, were taken to Montacute in 1947, with strict records being made as to where they had come from. These included mostly carpets and books, the latter being placed in the Library, which until then had been empty and desolate. Stourhead also lent some of its collection to Montacute.

Since those early days Montacute's collection has been added to and developed by a number of notable acquisitions. Many of these have been safeguarded for the house by the support of grant funders and fundraising. Today visitors can enjoy this remarkable, rich and unique collection, the result of a long and challenging project spanning many years, in its spectacular surroundings.

Above This fine maiolica dish came with the Sir Malcolm Stewart bequest (see p.35)

Left Borrowed books have bought the Library back to life

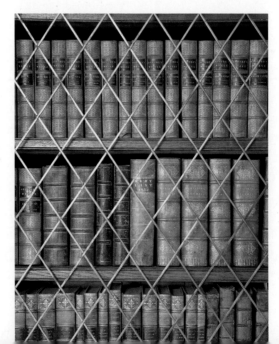

Right The Parlour and the
other principal rooms have
gradually been refurnished

Tapestries
(Donor: Stewart)

Some of the highlights of the collection are the textiles, which would have been vital for furnishing and decorating any great house in the 17th century. Acquired for Montacute through the generous bequest of Sir Malcolm Stewart, they are part of one of the first, and perhaps the finest, collections offered to the house.

Sir Malcolm was a businessman who made his fortune with the London Brick Company, which, in the 1920s, was said to be the largest brick-making company in the UK. A collector of antiques, mostly bought through the 'dealer-cum-decorator' Murray Acton-Adams, Sir Malcolm left his internationally recognised collection of furniture, tapestries and paintings to Montacute in his will in 1951 'in order that it may re-assume its former character as the stately home of an Englishman as distinct from the aspect of a museum'. The collection comprised objects that were probably grander than those which the Phelips family would have owned. However, Sir Malcolm's aims were unquestionably met, and the collection arrived at the house in 1960, after the death of his widow, Lady Stewart.

The stars of Sir Malcolm's bequest are without doubt the tapestries. Vital for warmth, required for privacy and enjoyed for decoration, the purchase of tapestries would have been a major investment for the Phelips family, and the 1638 inventory records the wealth of textiles in the house.

Of the five tapestries included in Sir Malcolm's bequest the finest by far is also the earliest. The *millefleurs* tapestry, representing a knight on horseback against a background of thousands of flowers, was woven in the French tapestry-making town of Tournai in 1477–9. It is one of the few surviving tapestries from the late 15th century, and its quality is comparable with any owned by King Henry VIII at Hampton Court.

Another late 15th-century tapestry is the Flemish *Eleventh Labour of Hercules: The Apples of the Hesperides,* which depicts scenes from the life of Hercules.

Above This late 15th-century Flemish tapestry depicts scenes from the life of Hercules

Opposite The rare tapestry of a knight on horseback against a background of flowers was woven in Tournai in 1477–9

Tapestries
(Donor: Stewart)

Further bequests from Sir Malcolm include two 16th-century tapestries showing religious scenes: *The Descent from the Cross* is from Brussels; and *The Virgin, St John the Baptist and St Claudius* was made in Germany.

The last, and latest, tapestry from the Stewart collection, *The Hunter,* is one of eight which together were called *La Nouvelle Tenture des Indes.* Designed in France around 1731, it is based on an earlier set made for Louis XIV at the famous Gobelins factory in Paris. Dated 1788, it is signed by the master weaver James Neilson, a Scotsman who worked at the Gobelins factory. The tapestry remains remarkably fresh and bright and adds a touch of exoticism to Montacute.

Right Detail of *The Hunter;* Gobelins tapestry, dated 1788

Opposite *The Descent from the Cross;* early 16th-century Brussels tapestry

Samplers
(Donor: Goodhart)

Textiles of many kinds were vital to the furnishing of an important 17th-century country house. As well as cushions, curtains, wall- and bed-hangings and table-coverings, the specialised form of the sampler was highly valued. These small items were considered of great importance; important enough to be listed in inventories of a house's contents or in a will.

Small embroidered items usually depicting letters of the alphabet or small designs, samplers were initially made by experienced embroiderers to record and share stitches and patterns. A 'sample' design would be embroidered on a narrow piece of fabric, often linen, to be eventually copied onto a more significant and valuable item of textile, such as a curtain or piece of clothing. Less experienced needleworkers used these to copy and practise their skills. Originally undertaken as a leisure activity by the mistress of a big house or her daughters, when needlework was considered to be a very important skill in upper-class families, the creation of samplers became increasingly educational. With the opening of many rural schools in the mid-19th century, and the Victorian desire to increase the people's level of basic numeracy and literacy, the design of samplers became much more structured, with rows upon rows of embroidered numbers and letters filling the blank pieces of linen. Also often incorporated were moral or religious texts, designed to teach or improve their creator.

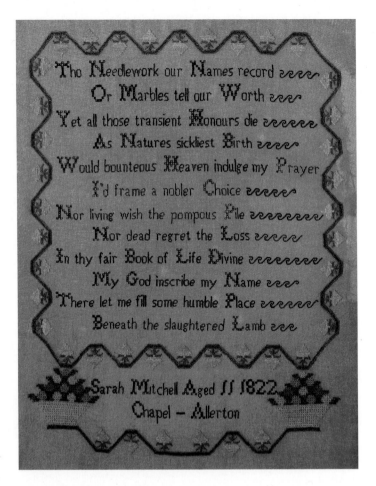

The first samplers were produced more than 400 years ago and are still popular today, with courses being run by organisations such as the Royal School of Needlework. Samplers tell us much about the development of technique and design in changing fashions of needlework. Now regarded as an art form, as such they mirror the society in which they were made and the influences and interests of those who created them.

One of the most important collections given to Montacute is an outstanding group of 130 samplers, dating from the early 17th to the 20th centuries. Bequeathed to the house in 1988 by

Above Dr Goodhart's internationally important collection of samplers began with his chance encounter with this example, dated 1822

Opposite left A band sampler, embroidered by Alice Jennings in 1692

Opposite right A spot sampler, embroidered by Elizabeth Branch in 1670

Dr Douglas Goodhart, this collection, mostly dating from the 17th century, is of international importance. Dr Goodhart was a doctor and anaesthetist, who, passing by an antique shop in Sussex in the 1950s, purchased a small sampler which had caught his eye. This sampler, made by an eleven-year-old girl called Sarah Mitchell in 1822, was bought by him 'to preserve it for the sake of the child, who had so painstakingly embroidered it'. From this chance beginning he became increasingly fascinated by this specialised form of textiles and, 32 years later, had collected around 300 samplers, one of the finest collections in the country.

Furniture
(Donor: Chester)

Montacute today houses some internationally important pieces of furniture, a collection which has been acquired since the Trust's first appeal in *The Times*.

Only a few pieces of original Phelips furniture survive: these include a set of six early 18th-century Queen Anne walnut armchairs with cane backs. Initially on loan from a member of the family, Commander Harry Phelips, they were purchased in 1980 and are now secure for permanent display.

The set of 18th-century chairs, settee and screen is of special interest. The gilt walnut frames set off the textile covers, the backs finely embroidered in 1722 with mythological scenes of figures dressed in classical robes set in 'chinoiserie' – European interpretation of Chinese – landscapes. The faces of the figures are worked on linen with tiny stitches and are very fine examples of the skill of the embroiderer. The seats are embroidered with flowers, it not being thought correct at the time to be seated on the image of a person. Originally from Chicheley Hall in Buckinghamshire, this important set was generously loaned from Major Chester, but was transferred to the Trust by HM Revenue and Customs in 2012.

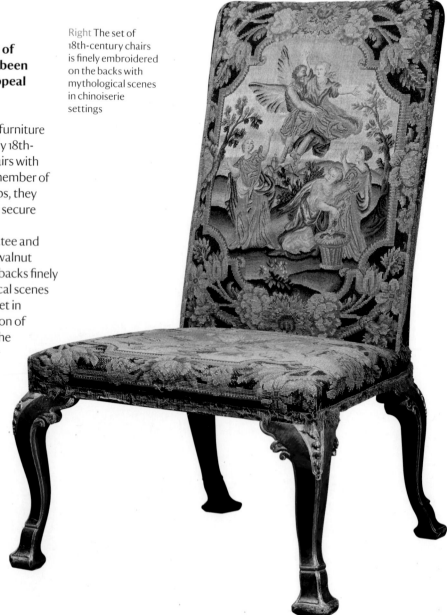

Right The set of 18th-century chairs is finely embroidered on the backs with mythological scenes in chinoiserie settings

Silver

A silver epergne, purchased by the National Trust in 2006, was a significant acquisition because it had once belonged to the Phelips family and is made in the shape of the family crest, a burning brazier. A type of centrepiece for a dinner table or sideboard, common in France and introduced to England in the early 18th century, the name comes from the French *épargner* (to save), and was used to save space on the table, as well as to save the trouble of passing several dishes individually. Commissioned by Edward Phelips from Thomas Pitts in 1781, although possibly not for Montacute itself, it is a fine example of the work of this renowned silversmith.

Another early loan, and subsequent bequest, to the house, from Mr J.C.B. Gamlen, was that of the massive oak bed. Decorated with the coats of arms of James I, Prince Frederick of the Palatinate and Henry, Prince of Wales, this enables the bed to be dated to 1612 and to the celebration of the marriage of Elizabeth, James's daughter, to Prince Frederick. The bed would have originally been shorter and lower, the fashion at the time being to sleep propped up on bolsters and pillows. It was later extended and made taller. Beds were a significant expense in Elizabethan times and often listed in wills.

Books

Two books in the collection stand apart from the others, which were brought in by the Trust from Brockhampton House in Herefordshire in 1947. A Phelips family bible in two volumes, bound in red calf and dated 1717, has a handwritten record of Phelips family births on the frontispiece. The second, considered to be the single most important volume in the house, is an 18th-century Phelips catalogue of the library. Its significance lies in the story it tells of the family's interests at the time and, as such, may well inform future acquisitions of items for the house.

Above left The oak four-poster bed was made in 1612 to celebrate the marriage of James I's daughter, Princess Elizabeth, to Prince Frederick of the Palatinate

Above The silver epergne (table centrepiece) was commissioned by Edward Phelips in 1781

The National Portrait Gallery partnership

Forty years after its acquisition by the National Trust, with low visitor numbers and no endowment or other source of income to fund the property, Montacute was in trouble.

The then Chair of the Trust's Properties Committee, Lord Rosse, had the idea of a possible partnership with the National Portrait Gallery and talks with the Gallery's Director at the time, (Sir) Roy Strong, led to the partnership that continues to flourish today. The collaboration offered the opportunity 'to show portraits in their original surroundings' and was regarded by Strong as 'one of the most important events in the Gallery's history' at the time.

The carefully selected portraits in the Long Gallery date from the 16th and early 17th centuries and in certain details, such as the rush matting on the floor, relate directly to their surroundings. They provide a glimpse of the life of the wealthy and influential in England around the time the house was built, not only in the lives of each sitter, but also in the way in which the paintings can be encountered and discussed while walking in the Gallery.

Painted portraits were initially only commissioned by the royal family and the elite at court; however, they were comparatively cheap and became increasingly popular amongst the wealthy and the 'middling sort' by the end of the 16th century. Far more money was spent on clothing, and it was through the detailed portrayal of jewels and expensive fabrics that the painter could show the sitter's wealth. During the reign of Queen Elizabeth I portraits began to incorporate symbols and allegorical imagery, in addition to details such as the sitter's age and the date of the painting; these provided further entertainment as the viewer could demonstrate their own education and ability to interpret the painting.

The partnership with the National Portrait Gallery has also brought portraits of some of the individuals who lived at Montacute back to the house, such as the paintings of Sir Robert Phelips in the Great Hall and Lord Curzon in the Curzon Bedroom.

Opposite *Mary, Lady Scudamore;* painted by Marcus Gheeraerts the younger, 1615 (National Portrait Gallery)

Right *King Charles I;* painted c.1616 (National Portrait Gallery)

Paintings
(Donor: Carmichael)

A major acquisition by the National Trust for Montacute was made in 2011, when a court portrait of King James VI of Scotland and I of England was purchased.

Thanks to the great generosity of a former volunteer at the house, Moira Carmichael, this important painting returned to the house, having been away for 30 years. Probably given by the King to Sir Edward Phelips, the builder of the house, perhaps in recognition of the role he played in the Guy Fawkes prosecution after the Gunpowder Plot, this portrait clearly places the Phelips family at the heart of the Stuart

court. Sold by the family in the 1980s, the painting disappeared from public view during the intervening years, re-emerging at auction in 2011.

One of a number of contemporary versions, this picture is based on a full-length pattern by John de Critz the Elder, for which payments are recorded in 1606 and 1607. De Critz came originally from Flanders, as did many of the most popular artists at the time, and rose to the post of 'Serjeant Painter', responsible for producing portraits and other paintings for the King. The return of this painting to Montacute is of great significance and shows, once again, that 'spirit of generosity' of people towards the house and its estate.

Opposite *King James I;* painted by John de Critz the Elder

Right *Sir William Heathcote, the Rev. William Heathcote and Major Vincent Hawkins Gilbert out hunting;* painted by Daniel Gardner, 1790 (Stewart bequest)

Far right *Anthony Francis Haldimand;* painted by Sir Thomas Lawrence, c.1798 (Stewart bequest)

Paintings
(Donor: Stewart)

The Trust has been fortunate to benefit from other gifts and bequests of paintings for display in the house. The extraordinary bequest of Sir Malcolm Stewart, which included the outstanding tapestries (see p.35), also comprised paintings of extremely high quality by such artists as Thomas Gainsborough, Sir Joshua Reynolds and Sir Thomas Lawrence. Paintings have also been lent from other National Trust houses. Ernest Cook, as well as gifting the money to save Montacute itself, bequeathed paintings to the house in his will.

The important collection of 40 portraits of the Phelips family are the only items never to have left the house, thanks to generations of the family who, despite times of financial difficulty, never included them in the various sales of items from their home. Displaying a complete run of the owners of Montacute since 1600, and vital to telling the story of the house, these had been on loan since 1931 and were eventually purchased thanks to grant funding in 1989.

Left *Susan Murrill, Mrs Henry Hill*; painted by Thomas Gainsborough, c.1750s

Opposite Possibly *Elizabeth Hamilton*; painted by Sir Joshua Reynolds, c.1754

The Garden

The garden at Montacute provides a glorious setting for the house.

It is one of the few Elizabethan garden structures surviving in England today. Its importance lies in its design, with the formal grid outlines of the house extending to the walls, terraces and other features of the garden to create a real sense of unity.

The development of the garden

Planned as one with the house and originally laid out at the same time, around 1600, there were formal areas on two sides of the house, with the other two containing the service buildings. Intended to be viewed both from the ground and from the house, the designed gardens are framed by the surrounding Somerset landscape.

The first detailed survey of the gardens dates from 1667 and indicates how they would have been used, for both leisure and the production of food or other domestic requirements. It includes details of the enclosed and highly ornamental courtyard entrance to the east, with its twinned structures, and the North Garden, with its raised walks and symmetrical design. Typical of this period, much of it survives today.

Whilst the planting and some of its other features have changed over the years, the basic form remains, perhaps in part due to periods of neglect, when the family was facing financially hard times. Any changes made were always sympathetic to the essence of the Elizabethan original, even if perhaps influenced by fashions of the time. The 18th century saw a revival of the garden under Edward Phelips V. When William Phelips and his wife Ellen moved into the house in the mid-19th century, they, together with the gardener Mr Pridham from her former home, created significant new garden designs, part of a conscious celebration of Tudor and Stuart gardens in England.

'A place gracious to enter, and that would tempt the visitor to remain.'

Avray Tipping, 1904

Left The house from
the North Garden

Right The East Court
borders

The East Court

The East Court today has its origins in its Elizabethan purpose of creating an impressive entrance befitting a house of such high status. Its façade of architectural details and quantities of window glass were designed to inspire awe and reverence in visitors.

The East Court is enclosed on three sides by balustraded walls of Ham stone, decorated with obelisks, with the fourth side leading to the house steps, terrace and entrance. Originally an austere gravelled area with a central stone pathway, it was softened by a lawn. The remarkable lodges form a dominant feature of the East Court and reflect the house in architectural style and splendour. Each had a large chimney and upper floor. It was believed that they were matched by a grand gatehouse, which had been demolished by the 18th century.

The East Court was probably turned into a garden and re-designed when the new West Drive was created, with the whole central area laid to grass and surrounded by a gravel path and flower beds. The garden underwent a major remodelling by William and Ellen Phelips after 1845, when they moved into Montacute. This included reducing the main lawn to grass strips along the three sides, and interplanting the area with Irish yews. The central section was laid to gravel around a new fountain basin. The terrace was softened with climbing plants on the columns and large pots of plants. The fountain had been removed and the area returfed by the time Montacute was bequeathed to the National Trust in 1931.

Aware that the garden needed more work than it could provide in-house, the Trust sought advice from Vita Sackville-West, the writer and gardener, on the design and presentation of the East Court. Vita's first visit to Montacute was in 1947. Unable to pay Vita for her expertise, the Trust recompensed her in petrol coupons, valuable in post-war times. Vita advised the planting of 'LARGE MASSES' in the borders, with yellow, orange and bronze colours to be 'ruthlessly eliminated' as they clashed with Ham stone. Instead mauve, deep purple, blue and silver grey were felt to be much more in keeping.

In 1950 further advice was sought from Phyllis Reiss, noted for her thoughtful approach to planting at her nearby garden at Tintinhull House (now also in the care of the National Trust). She supervised the replanting of the Court, using the planting scheme and colour palette proposed by Vita. Phyllis was determined that the border should 'form the best possible frame for the magnificence of the house', believing that 'Ham stone eats up colour excepting showy colours'. She continued to help each week at Montacute until at least 1955, and the beds today are still planted following her colours and design, with symmetrical arrangements of bold blocks of colour to create a repeating rhythm along each border. Phyllis was given a transistor radio as thanks for her help, a gift she much appreciated.

Left above The East Court terrace

This picture The East Court from above

The North
Garden

The North Garden, a large square area on two levels with an upper terrace surrounding a lower sunken garden, is a rare Elizabethan survival of a privy garden, a high-status area only for use by family and guests.

This part of the garden was built at the same time as the house and was designed to be seen from above. There are now substantial yew hedges along the north and west edges, and an open terrace looks out over the park to the east. The raised walks look down onto the regular lines of round-clipped Irish yews and its four symmetrical lawns with gravel paths leading to the large ornamental central fountain basin.

A banqueting house once stood in the corner of the North Garden overlooking the park. This high-status garden room, away from the main house, commanded views over the deer-park, an important asset for an Elizabethan gentleman when the sport of coursing (the chasing of deer by hounds) was considered a great and necessary entertainment. The building was also used for serving delicacies to the family after dinner.

The round-clipped Irish yews in the North Garden

The North Garden from above

Few alterations were made in the 18th century, with the exception of the building of an ice-house set into the north-west corner of the raised terrace. A large brick-lined chamber with a domed roof, and most of its volume lying underground, its dressed stone doorway signified both its ornamental and functional uses.

When William and Ellen Phelips moved into Montacute after 1845, they remodelled the garden. Their ambitious plans included a new elaborate layout of the parterres and intricate beds in the garden, with a formal structure of quartered beds around a central fountain basin. A previous central mound and original pond had already disappeared. The Irish yew trees they planted around the parterres became one of the defining features of the gardens. The hedges, planted at the same time, developed from their original rectangular form to the current 'cloud' shape, for which the garden is known today.

The present Orangery was probably built by 1840 on the site of a former building. The use of obelisks linked it with the Elizabethan origins of the garden.

By the turn of the 20th century, the garden, with its large, labour-intensive areas, was suffering from impoverishment and neglect. The intricate parterres had been simplified to four tiered beds with one at the centre of each quarter. The North Garden was thought to be 'a trifle dull' by Gertrude Jekyll during a visit in 1920. The Royal Horticultural Society provided expertise during the 1940s, and Vita Sackville-West offered advice on the North Garden as part of her 1947 commission.

The date of the rose border is unclear, but it appears on a photograph of c.1860. Border widths and planting schemes changed between 1930 and 1950. Vita Sackville-West made recommendations, as did Graham Stuart Thomas before his appointment as the first Gardens Adviser to the Trust in 1955. The rose border is regarded as an important early example of his work with the Trust.

The West and South Drives

Today, the straight, tree-lined West Drive provides an important first glimpse of the house to visitors passing on the road through the village.

It passes through a formal gateway, with gate piers topped with the Phelips 'basket of flames' crest. The original entrance to the house was from the east off the Ilchester road until about 1780, when Edward Phelips V reorientated the house during his extensive programme of re-design. He added his new Clifton Maybank front onto the west front of Montacute, at the age of 60, and created a serpentine drive with a 'landscaped' approach from the west.

'On the 19th of December I began Forming a New Road to the West Front of Montacute house… [a] very great and Arduous Undertaking at My advanced season of life.'

Edward Phelips V

When William and Ellen moved into Montacute in 1845, they made plans to reconfigure the West Drive to create the current straight approach. The gateway replaced the earlier one at the beginning of the sweeping drive. The plans included a three-tiered avenue of alternate Deodar Cedars and Cedars of Lebanon, Monkey Puzzles and Monterey Pines, and an inner line of Irish Yews with 15 pairs in total. Only the yews survive more or less intact. The current stable block was built as part of this West Drive work, around 1850. An all-weather tennis court was built nearby, but this was removed in 1949, when the area returned to service use.

Under National Trust ownership, Graham Stuart Thomas created a deep shrub border on the south-east corner of the West Drive in the late 1960s. The great storm of 1990 caused loss and damage to several mature trees along the drive, many dating from the 19th century. During the Second World War, when Montacute was requisitioned by the War Department, many of the drives through the property were tarmacked over, with repairs only being made in 1972.

A second entrance, known as the South Drive, also led to the west front of the house. It was first recorded on an 1807 map as the main service entrance. By the mid-19th century it had become a secondary, but ornamental, approach to the house. Some remnants of the Californian redwoods planted by William and Ellen, and cut down in the Second World War, still remain.

This increase in status warranted a new gateway and lodge. Its location in the centre of the village was the first indication of the importance of the family who lived in the house. The South Lodge was given the same architectural treatment as the lodges in the East Court and may have used materials from its original gatehouse. The north half was built about 1770, and the second half dates from about 1851.

Opposite The West Drive

The Cedar Lawn

This large, rectangular area of garden contrasts with the formally designed and ornamental East Court and North Garden. It is simple in its design, with gravel paths around a large lawn, enclosed on three sides by a high yew hedge and with four large trees.

The fourth side looks out over a low stone wall to the parkland. In the south-west corner an arcaded summerhouse provides a point of architectural interest and shelter from the rain.

This was originally a service area and was recorded in 1774 as Pig's Wheatle Orchard. By 1825 it was referred to as 'a bowling green'. Its current enclosed character is believed to date to the mid-19th century. Laid out as a lawn, it probably had many more trees than it does today. The distinctive yew hedges were recorded in *Country Life* magazine in 1898 as being smooth and formal.

The summerhouse, first clearly recorded in 1903, is likely to have incorporated stone from the banqueting house, which previously stood in the North Garden. The current pediment and balustrade were added by Lord Curzon in the early 20th century and display a central shield decorated with the Strode family arms, probably from nearby Barrington Court. Curzon's additions were much disapproved of: it was said that the shield and other materials had been found in 'a lot of old rubbish in the carpenters yard'.

After the Second World War, when Montacute was returned to the Trust by the War Department, there was a reduction in labour available in the garden. Lawns had become meadows, scythed annually, and Mr J. Wilson, the RHS gardens adviser, suggested that the Irish yew hedges be left untrimmed to reduce labour. The development of the 'cloud' hedge, so characteristic of the garden today, dates back to this period.

Above The Cedar Lawn

The Cut-Flower Border and Service Block

Behind the yew hedge lies the Cut-Flower Border, which runs the length of the Cedar Lawn and was one of the original service entrances to the house.

This servants' path was planted with flowers for cutting and still produces them for the house today. The fifteen fan-trained fig trees were planted along the back wall of the border. Historically, they were grown more for their foliage than for the fruit they produced.

The Cut-Flower Border wall is the back of the service block (now the Trust's restaurant and shop). A 1667 survey described the area to the south of the house as the 'large Woodyard and necessary buildings for Daryes Washing Brewing and Bakeing, a Pigeon house'. The current service block was recorded in this location by 1774, and its layout was adapted in the mid-19th century, the area being known as Laundry Court by 1887. It has been regularly adapted, as is often the case to meet changing needs, and at one time extended to the house itself, the outline of the two-storey pitched-roof building still being visible on the south side of the house.

Right The Cut-Flower Border provides colourful decoration for the house

The Pillar Garden and Kitchen Garden

The Pillar Garden, a small secluded space at the southern end of the Cedar Lawn, was created by Constance Louisa Fane, the second wife of William Robert Phelips, in about 1900.

It is separated from the lawn by an arcade of yews and features free-standing classical columns with beds of ornamental planting and striking yucca plants, which were replanted by the Trust around 1950 to a design by Graham Stuart Thomas.

To the west of the Topiary Garden was the former Kitchen Garden of the house, situated in the current visitor car-park. In its mid-19th-century heyday the substantial vinery, which produced surplus grapes selling at 1s 6d/pound in 1843, was complemented by pits and frames, all heated by a hot-water system. By 1887 all the glasshouses had been relocated to a sophisticated glass yard planted with fruit trees around its perimeter (now the overflow car-park), and included peach houses and pineapple, melon and cucumber pits. Here was grown most of the produce for the house, with exotic fruit and flowers like grapes and orchids suitable for a household of Montacute's status. A recollection of the Kitchen Garden in the late 19th century recalls that 'in the first kitchen garden were two circular fishponds' and a cut-flower border 'full of those lovely double pink primroses, pink cushions of scent'. However, by 1962 the area had become a meadow and, a few years later, the visitor car-park.

Right **The Pillar Garden**

Parkland

Montacute's nationally important parkland tells the story of the evolution of the English landscape over 1,000 years.

An evolving landscape

Designed both to frame the house and garden, and to enhance the views out, the relationship between them is hugely important. The parkland today holds clues to layers of history going back to Roman and medieval times.

In the Phelips family's time the parkland underwent three main phases of design, each generation acknowledging the original formal layout rather than creating a completely new design. When Sir Edward Phelips I built the house, his early park laid the foundations for all future developments. Although concentrating his wealth on the building of the house and garden, a small park was probably created to the east. Sir Edward also acquired the medieval deer-park from the former priory, dissolved by Henry VIII in the 1530s.

The second phase began when Edward Phelips V inherited in 1750. Creating a long avenue of trees in the park to the east of the house, which framed a bridge over an informal lake and a rustic grotto, Edward was perhaps influenced by the classically inspired 'landscape style'. Made fashionable by 'Capability' Brown in the 18th century, this moved away from the formality of the Elizabethan design. In the wider landscape Edward built the Prospect Tower on St Michael's Hill.

In the mid-19th century William and Ellen significantly increased the size of the parkland. The planting of trees, the removal of the bridge over the pond and the straightening of the West Drive were much more in keeping with the formal style of the house and garden.

Main Park

Once comprising farmland, the earliest ridge-and-furrow earthworks dating from the 13th century, the main parkland today mostly reflects the character of the 19th-century design.

It shows little evidence of its 18th-century landscaping, the only remaining feature being the long double Lime Avenue running east from the house and the 'ha-ha' ditch, which prevented livestock in the parkland from wandering into the garden without obstructing the view. Gone are the serpentine lake, its stone bridge and the grotto.

In the early 19th century much of the southern area of the park was still arable strips. The land to the north had become pasture, which William and Ellen converted to parkland, as well as significantly extending it. Most of the trees which survive today are from this period. They also removed the pond and other 18th-century parkland features. At this time the estate covered 1,748 acres, compared to only 303 acres in 1929 when the house was put on the market.

When the Trust acquired Montacute in 1931, the parkland was in poor condition, a result of years of financial difficulties for the family. During the Second World War a large camp of 34 Nissen huts, served by electricity and telephones, was built to the east of the house, the foundations only being removed in 1948.

Opposite Enjoying the house and park in autumn

Hornhay Orchard and Wellham's Brook

Hornhay Orchard, an area next to the North Garden, was one of several orchards planted by Sir Edward, mainly to the west and south of the formal garden.

Its ornamental fruit trees, such as cherry, pear and plum, were planted nearest to the house, most visible by family and guests. Further away, the planting became more functional, with eating and cider apples. In the 19th century Hornhay was consolidated with other small areas of orchard to create the extensive area remaining today.

Although still evident from aerial photographs, the orchards were not cultivated during the Second World War and fell out of use. The Trust, however, started to replant Hornhay in the late 20th century and continues today. The Orchard is important for the views from the house and for the remains of medieval ridge-and-furrow cultivation, which remain underneath. To the north-west of Hornhay Orchard is the area of Wellham's Brook and Mill Copse, the latter the site of Odcombe Flour Mill, a water mill since at least the 15th century. The tall, three-storey building was demolished in the 1950s, but its mill race, the channel which conducted water to the mill, and millpond remain. The picturesque quality of this area has a tranquil atmosphere, distinct from other areas of the park.

The Old Park, Ladies' Walk and St Michael's Hill

The Old Park belonged to a former monastic priory and was bought by Sir Edward in 1608. A discrete area, slightly apart from the main designed landscape, its medieval deer-park was highly valued by Sir Edward as a visible sign of his wealth and status.

Around its perimeter is Ladies' Walk, an undulating path through Park Covert. Planting here began in the 18th century with the picturesque terraced walk we know today, including its gothic arch over the spring in the Old Park below, designed a century later. The woodland planting is of predominantly broadleaved species such as beech. The dramatic ridgeline, which breaks in the planting, gives wide views to the house, village and beyond. As an important part of the wider landscape design little has changed, with the exception of the growth of the village. This circular walk returns through the Old Park, passing close by to two sweet chestnut trees, the oldest trees on the estate.

St Michael's Hill, directly overlooking the village, has been an important part of the greater landscape composition around the house since it was built. Indeed it gave the village its name, the Latin for its distinctive hill being *mons acutus*. The most archaeologically significant area within the Trust's ownership at Montacute, its earliest remains are from a medieval motte and bailey castle, built by Robert, Count of Mortain, half-brother to William the Conqueror. The 11th-century St Michael's Chapel built on its summit was demolished in the 16th century. Over the ruins of the chapel Edward Phelips V built the Prospect Tower and marked his achievement with a stone dated 1760.

Opposite above **The house from St Michael's Hill**

Opposite below left **Prospect Tower and St Michael's Hill from the house**

Opposite below right **Prospect Tower on St Michael's Hill**

The Future

The Trust faces major conservation challenges at Montacute, in both the house and exterior landscape.

The Elizabethan building design, together with the materials used in its creation, has resulted in structural problems in the house, many of which began in the 1860s, when the original stone tiles on the roof were replaced with Welsh slates. Not only did this affect the visual unity of the house within its setting, but it also changed the structural balance of the roof's design. A major programme of conservation, which began in 1982 and required re-opening the stone quarry at Ham Hill to provide the material, is still ongoing. The huge increase in the number of people visiting the property since it was acquired by the Trust also causes wear to other areas of the estate. The Trust's challenge is to work with these changes whilst still retaining the integrity of the original.

The Trust is also working hard to reinstate areas of the property whose original character has been lost. Historic varieties of fruit trees are being planted in Hornhay Orchard and the 18th-century parkland design is being re-established. Strengthening the unity of different elements of the estate – house, collection, garden and parkland – is of huge importance.

This much-loved property has a long association with the village of Montacute, and the close links between them encourage the sense of a communal landscape, to be enjoyed and cherished by all.

Below Montacute starred in the BBC adaptation of Hilary Mantel's *Wolf Hall*